ZOO ANIMALS IN THE WILD

LION

JINNY JOHNSON

ILLUSTRATED BY MICHAEL WOODS

W

FRANKLIN WATTS
LONDON • SYDNEY

An Appleseed Editions book

First published in 2006 by Franklin Watts
338 Euston Road, London NW1 3BH

Franklin Watts Australia
Hachette Children's Books
Level 17/207 Kent St, Sydney, NSW 2000

© 2006 Appleseed Editions

Created by Appleseed Editions Ltd, Well House,
Friars Hill, Guestling, East Sussex TN35 4ET

Designed by Helen James
Edited by Mary-Jane Wilkins
Illustrated by Michael Woods

ISBN 0 7496 6733 8

Dewey Classification: 599.757

A CIP catalogue for this book is available from the British Library

Photographs by Alamy (James Gritz), Robert E. Barber, Getty Images (Adrian Bailey / Aurora,
Skip Brown, Beverly Joubert / National Geographic, Timothy G. Laman / National Geographic,
Michael K. Nichols, Norbert Rosing / National Geographic, jonathan & angela scott, Manoj Shah,
Cameron Spencer, Justin Sullivan)

Printed and bound in Thailand

Contents

Lions and lionesses 4

Teeth, paws and claws 6

A lion pride 8

At home in the wild 10

At home in the zoo 12

A lion's day 14

Feeding time 16

Lion babies 18

Growing up 20

Playtime 22

Keeping in touch 24

Growing up 26

Lion fact file 28

Words to remember 30

Index 32

Lions and lionesses

Lions are among the most magnificent of all creatures. These big, strong cats have a large head, sturdy legs and a long tail tipped with a tuft of hair. Their fur is a deep golden colour.

Male lions are larger and more powerful than females. The male has a mane of hair around his neck and shoulders. This mane becomes fuller and darker in colour as the lion grows older. Some old lions have black manes. Female lions are called lionesses.

Lions are some of the most popular animals in zoos. Most large zoos keep lions. There are hundreds of lions living in zoos and safari parks all over the world.

The male lion's thick mane helps protect his head and neck from sharp claws when he fights with other males.

A lion often swishes its tufted tail back and forth to drive away annoying flies.

Teeth, paws and claws

Big, curved teeth and powerful, clawed paws are a lion's main weapons for catching food and fighting enemies.

A lion's front teeth are very sharp and can be as much as 6 cm long — that's about as long as a grown-up's finger.

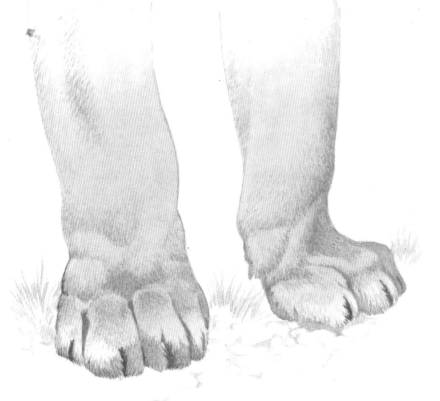

Most of the time
a lion keeps its claws
pulled back, out of
the way. But when
a lion wants to
scratch something
or attack prey it
puts its claws out.

The claws can be pulled
back into special covers
called sheaths. This stops
them getting blunt as the
lion walks around.

Every lion has a
slightly different
pattern of spots
above and at the base of
its whiskers.

A lion pride

Lions are the only cats, big or small, that live in groups. A lion family is called a pride. The pride is made up of a group of females, their young, and a few males.

A pride may contain only four or five lions or as many as 30 or more. Larger prides live in areas where there is plenty of food.

Living in a pride makes it easier to take care of the young animals. The females in a pride look after the cubs and often do most of the hunting together.

Most zoos aren't big enough to manage a whole pride of lions, but they do try to keep lions in small groups. Lions aren't happy living by themselves.

The male lions defend the pride against other males. If a stranger comes too near, the male lions attack and drive it away.

The lionesses in a pride often go hunting together.

At home in the wild

Most wild lions live in Africa. The lion is often called the king of the jungle, but lions usually live in open grassland, not in forest and jungle.

Male lions guard the pride's territory.
They can smell if strangers have been in the area.

Young lions and lionesses are good climbers and like to rest on branches. Full-grown males don't climb much – they are too heavy.

Lions need to live near fresh water so they can have a drink every day.

A few lions live in India, but only in protected areas called reserves.

Every pride of lions has its own special area, called a territory. There must be plenty of prey animals in the territory so the lions have enough to eat. There must be water, too, and hiding places for young cubs. Lions often stay in the same territory for many years.

At home in the zoo

Very few zoos now keep lions in cages.
Lions are big animals and they need
plenty of room to move around.

A good zoo makes sure its lions have rocks and other places where they can lie and doze during the day. They need trees or apparatus to climb and somewhere to hide away when they don't feel like being stared at.

Most zoos give lions an indoor den where it is easy for visitors to see the animals up close through the glass.

Wild lions don't eat every day so most zoos leave their lions hungry one day a week. It's easy for zoo lions to get fat.

A lion's day

You might think that lions are lazy.
They sleep for as much as 20 hours a day!
The rest of the time they hunt, defend
their territory and groom each other.

Lions sleep a lot for a good
reason. Finding food is
difficult and takes a lot
of energy. The more a lion
moves around, the hungrier
he gets. He may catch
something to eat only once
every two or three days.
Resting is a good way to
make a meal last longer.

Lions yawn when they are
nervous or anxious as well
as when they are sleepy.

14

Zoo lions sleep just as much as lions in the wild. When you go to see them, they'll nearly always be taking a nap – unless it's feeding time!

Lions groom each other to remove dirt, blood and insects from their fur. Grooming is also a good way of showing friendship.

Feeding time

Lions catch and eat other animals. They can run fast, but only for short distances. So they sneak up close to their prey before making a high-speed dash and pounce. Several members of the pride, usually females, hunt together and the whole pride shares the kill.

A lioness watches her prey carefully before slowly creeping closer.

When a lioness is near enough to her prey, she leaps on to its back to bring it to the ground for the kill.

Large animals, such as wildebeest and zebras, are the favourite prey of lions. But they also hunt smaller creatures, and even steal prey from other hunters. A big lion may eat 45 kilos of meat in one meal – that's like eating 200 big steaks in one go. But then the lion won't eat again for a week.

Zoo lions don't have to catch their food. They are given meat and some bones to chew most days. A lion's tongue has a very rough surface, which helps it scrape meat from bones.

Lion babies

A lioness gives birth to between two and five cubs at a time. She keeps them in a safe den away from the rest of the pride for the first few weeks. During this time the cubs feed only on their mother's milk.

When the cubs are born they are blind and completely helpless. They weigh around two kilos — about the same as two bags of sugar.

A lion cub can feed from any lioness in the pride, not just its own mum.

The cubs' eyes open when they are between 10 and 15 days old. They grow their first baby teeth at about three weeks.

A mother lion moves her cubs to a new hiding place every three or four days. She moves them one by one, carrying them in her mouth.

The keepers keep a close eye on mum and cubs when a lioness gives birth in a zoo. She doesn't need to worry about keeping her babies safe.

Growing up

When the cubs are about six weeks old, they start moving around their den. Now they are ready to meet the rest of the family. They're nervous at first, but soon get used to the other lions.

Lion cubs don't sleep all day like grown-up lions.
They like to run and jump.

Cubs feed on their mother's milk for a year or more, but start to eat some meat as well at three months. Soon they start following mum when she goes hunting, but they stay well out of the way. The cubs grow their adult teeth when they are between 9 and 12 months old.

When a playful cub is too mischievous his mother may give him a gentle cuff with her paw to say, 'that's enough'.

Lion cubs learn to hunt their own food by watching their mother – from a safe distance.

Playtime

Lion cubs spend most of their waking hours playing. But play is serious business for young lions. As they play, they are practising the skills they will need later when hunting and fighting.

Cubs practise their hunting skills on each other at first.

Young lions in zoos are given plenty of playthings to keep them busy and interested – even a roll of cardboard can be lots of fun.

While the older lions snooze, the cubs pounce on their tails and risk a cuff for their cheekiness. They try to catch insects and chase leaves or anything else that catches their eye. Sometimes the cubs play with the adults, but more often they play with each other.

Play fights are good exercise and help cubs grow stronger.

Keeping in touch

Lions in a pride need to keep in touch, like any family members. Everyone knows that lions roar, but did you realize that their roars can be heard as far as eight kilometres away?

Lions usually roar at night. They do this to contact other pride members, who might be away looking for food. A lion's roar also tells other lions how big and strong it is.

Lions can tell the roars of other pride members from those of strangers.

This snarling face, with bared teeth, means 'keep away from me'.

Lions leave scent messages around their territory by scratching trees or spraying liquid from a gland near the tail. They also do a regular check – sniffing to find out who else has passed by.

Male lions do most of the marking, and they also patrol their territory.

Growing up

Lion cubs have a lot to learn. It takes them several years to learn how to catch prey and defend themselves.

Cubs learn to hunt by watching their mother. By the time a cub is a year old it can kill some prey and by the age of two it can hunt alone.

Young lions pay close attention to everything their parents do.

Once a young lion can find its own food it can survive away from the pride. Many females stay with their mother's pride, but some leave and form new prides. Males always leave the pride where they were born.

Young male lions usually live alone or with other young males for a few years before finding a new pride to join.

Lion fact file

Here is some more information about lions.
Your mum or dad might like to read this,
or you could read these pages together.

A lion is a mammal. It belongs to the cat family and
like all cats it is a carnivore, which means it eats meat.

Where lions live

There are lions in parts of east, central, west and southern Africa,
south of the Sahara Desert. They live in savanna areas in countries
such as Senegal, Angola, Kenya and Tanzania. There used to be
lions in Asia too, but the only lions left there now are in the
protected Gir Forest reserve in India.

Lion numbers

Conservation organizations believe that the number of lions in
the wild has gone down by as much as half over the last 20 years.
Large areas of their habitat have been destroyed and animals
are still killed by poachers, although this is against the law.
The World Conservation Union (IUCN) lists the African lion
as vulnerable. The Asiatic lion is listed as endangered – there
are only about 250 left.

Size

A male lion is between 1.7 and 2.5 metres long, with a tail measuring about a metre. He weighs between 150 and 250 kilograms. Females are smaller – between 1.4 and 1.75 metres long, with a tail measuring between 70 centimetres and a metre. Females weigh about 120 kilograms.

Find out more

Check out these websites

Big Cat Rescue
http://www.bigcatrescue.org/lion.htm

Smithsonian National Zoological Park
http://nationalzoo.si.edu/animals/greatcats/lionfacts.cfm

San Diego Zoo
http://www.sandiegozoo.org/animalbytes/t-lion.html

African Wildlife Foundation
http://www.awf.org/wildlives/148

Words to remember

gland

A part of the body that makes a special substance, such as fluid for marking territory.

mammal

A warm-blooded animal, usually with four legs and some hair on its body. Female mammals feed their babies with milk from their own bodies.

mane

The long hair that grows round a male lion's head and neck.

patrol

Walking round and round territory, watching out for danger or enemies.

prey

An animal that is hunted and eaten by another animal.

pride
A group of lions that live in the same territory.
A pride usually has several related females
with their young and one or more male lions.

safari park
A park where lions and other animals
can live in the open, not in cages.

sheaths
The special covers that protect
a lion's claws when they are
not using them.

territory
The area where an animal spends
most of its time and finds its food.

wildebeest
A large, plant-eating animal,
which lives in Africa.

Index

claws 5, 6, 7
cubs 8, 11, 18, 19, 20, 21, 26

eyes 19

food 8, 14, 16, 17, 18, 21, 27

grooming 15

hunting 8, 9, 14, 16, 17, 21, 22, 26

lion numbers 28

mane 4, 5

paws 6, 7, 21
playing 21, 22, 23
prey 7, 11, 16, 17, 26

roaring 24

scent 25
size 29
sleeping 13, 14, 15, 20

tail 4, 5, 23, 29
teeth 6, 19, 21, 25
territory 10, 11, 14, 25
tongue 17

yawning 14